The Answers You Seek

Are Within

Divine Guidance

Messages from the Angels

Guidance and Inspiration from Divine Messengers

Amanda M Clarke

Koru Lifestylist

KORU (Maori:NZ)
A symbol of spiritual growth and spiritual connection.

"Messages from the Angels" by Amanda M. Clarke is a transformative journey into the realm of celestial wisdom, guided by the ethereal presence of angels. This unique book combines Amanda's profound insights with stunning AI-generated illustrations of the 34 archangels, creating a visual and spiritual feast that enhances the reader's experience. Each page is adorned with captivating images that bring your angelic messages to life, making "Messages from the Angels" not only a guide but a work of art. Designed for seekers of spiritual guidance, this book offers empowering, soothing, and enlightening messages from the angelic realm, making it a must-have for anyone looking to deepen their connection with the divine.

Copyright © 2024 by Koru Lifestylist

All rights reserved. All content, materials, and intellectual property in this book or any other platform owned by Koru Lifestylist are protected by copyright laws. This includes text, images, graphics, videos, audio, software, and any other form of content that may be produced by Koru Lifestylist.

No part of this content may be reproduced, distributed, or transmitted in any form or by any means without the prior written permission of Koru Lifestylist. This means that you cannot copy, reproduce, or use any of the content in this book for commercial or personal purposes without the express written consent of Koru Lifestylist.

Unauthorized use of any copyrighted material owned by Koru Lifestylist may result in legal action being taken against you. Koru Lifestylist reserves the right to pursue all available legal remedies against any individual or entity found to be infringing on its copyright.

In summary, Koru Lifestylist © 2024 holds exclusive rights to all the content produced by it, and any unauthorized use of such content will result in legal action.

Introduction to the Angels

Welcome to "Messages from the Angels: Guidance and Inspiration from Divine Messengers," where we explore the celestial advice of 34 angels whose names and narratives enrich various mystical and esoteric traditions. This book seeks to bridge the ancient with the contemporary, offering insights that resonate with seekers of all backgrounds.

In the realm of spiritual and mystical studies, the identification and roles of angels have evolved significantly over millennia. While some angelic names are well-known and widely acknowledged across multiple religious doctrines, others originate from lesser-known apocryphal texts and modern esoteric interpretations. The proliferation of angelic names in various new age texts highlights an ongoing fascination with divine intermediaries but also introduces challenges related to the authenticity and origins of these beings.

Many of the angelic names you will encounter here are derived from deep interpretations of ancient scriptures, creative extrapolations, or are innovations of recent centuries. These names have surfaced in texts that are not always part of the canonical religious traditions but are nonetheless revered in certain circles for their spiritual significance.

As we delve into the messages of each angel featured in this book, it is important to note that the recognition and acceptance of their names and roles can vary considerably across different spiritual traditions. This diversity reflects the rich tapestry of human belief and the myriad ways in which cultures seek to understand the celestial realm.

Through "Messages from the Angels," we invite you to open your heart to the wisdom of these divine messengers, embracing the guidance they provide as you navigate your spiritual journey.

How to use this book

STEP ONE: CLEAR YOUR BOOKS ENERGY

Since your book is a sensitive instrument and has been through many hands to reach you, you will need to clear it of any energy it may have absorbed. Steps One and Two only need to be completed every so often when the energies of the book become clogged.

It is a good idea to ground yourself first before clearing the book. Do this by sitting on a standard kitchen chair, with your feet comfortably flat on the floor. You can do this with shoes on, but it is better in bare feet. Better still, stand barefoot on the ground in the open, this will ensure all energies will be fully grounded out into the nothingness of the earth.

Hold the book in the palm of your non-dominant hand as this is the hand that receives energy.

Form a fist with your other hand and knock on the book once with your fist sending all energies from the book to the ground and into nothingness.

This clears out the old energy and the book is now blank and is ready to be imbued with your energy.

STEP TWO: CONSECRATE THE BOOK

Flip through the pages of the book ensuring you touch every page with your thumb, fingers or hand. This will start infusing it with your energy.

Hold the book in your dominant hand up to your heart and think about the prayers or intentions you would like to infuse the book with. For example, you may say to yourself in your minds-eye or aloud:-

"I ask that all of my readings with this book be accurate and specific, and bring blessings to everyone involved. Please help me stay centred in my higher self so that I may hear, see, feel, and know the messages that wish to come through these readings"

You may wish to keep your book wrapped in a silk scarf or unique bag as this will keep other people's energies from transferring to your pages.

STEP THREE: INVOKE THE ARCHANGELS
a. Find yourself a safe and comfortable place, somewhere quiet and you feel at peace.

b. Take 3 deep breaths to clear the mind. Inhale deeply through your nose, exhale through your lips and close your eyes.

c. Ask the Archangels to be present around you. Visualise a bright white orb of light surrounding you. Ask out aloud or in your mind's eye:-
"Archangels, I ask that you stay by my side and watch over me during this reading, ensuring that only God's love and wisdom come through. I trust that you will guide me toward the best outcome. Thank you for your presence and guidance"

STEP FOUR: ASK A QUESTION
Think of a question you would like the answer to. If you're giving a reading for someone else, ask him or her to either think of or verbalize a question. The archangels hear your thoughts, so you need not voice your queries aloud.

STEP FIVE: CHOOSE A PAGE
Take a deep breath and open your eyes.
Flip through the book. You may flip backward and forward using your thumbs or any method you choose. You may just open the book to a page, or keep flipping through the pages until you feel the sense to stop. You may even hear in your thoughts "Stop," or a page may just grab.

STEP SIX: THE ARCHANGELS MESSAGE
Read the passage on the archangel and the message they wish to convey to you. Take a moment and reflect on the message. Pay attention to any thoughts or feelings that come to you, as they are a part of the answer. Each Archangel comes with a 'Mantra' which you can say aloud or to yourself, calling upon the archangel to guide you.

JOURNAL PAGES
Write your thoughts, and feelings or scribble doodles at will. If you open a reading page on a blank page, this can mean that you already know the answer within yourself. By doodling or writing at will, you will feel and/or inscribe the message your guardian angels wish you to know.... enjoy this book!

The Answers You Seek

Are Within

Archangel Jegudiel's divine message is one of perseverance and strength in the face of adversity. The angel reminds us that we are capable of overcoming any obstacle, and that our challenges are opportunities for growth and transformation.

Jegudiel also encourages us to trust in our intuition and inner guidance, as these can lead us to our true purpose and calling. By listening to our inner voice and following our heart's desires, we can find meaning and fulfillment in our lives.

Finally, Jegudiel reminds us of the importance of gratitude and appreciation for the blessings in our lives. When we focus on what we have rather than what we lack, we open ourselves up to more abundance and joy.

Overall, Archangel Jegudiel's message is one of perseverance, intuition, and gratitude. The angel reminds us to trust in our inner strength and guidance, find meaning and purpose in our lives, and cultivate a spirit of gratitude and appreciation.

Archangel Jegudiel Mantra...
"I am strong, I am resilient, I am guided by my intuition, and I am grateful for all of my blessings."

By repeating this mantra, you can connect with Jegudiel's energy and tap into your own inner strength and resilience. This mantra can also help you to trust in your intuition and guidance, and cultivate a spirit of gratitude for all of the blessings in your life.

Archangel Zathael comes with a message of transformation, growth, and spiritual evolution. This powerful angel reminds you that change is a natural part of life and that it's time to embrace the opportunities for growth and transformation that are presenting themselves to you.

Zathael also reminds you to trust in your own intuition and inner guidance, as well as the guidance of the divine realm. You are being guided towards your highest good and towards fulfilling your soul's purpose.

Finally, Zathael encourages you to let go of any limiting beliefs or negative patterns that are holding you back. It's time to step into your power and to embrace your true potential. Trust in the process of transformation and know that you are supported every step of the way.

Archangel Zathael Mantra...

"Archangel Zathael, I embrace the opportunities for growth and transformation that are presenting themselves to me. I trust in my own intuition and inner guidance, as well as the guidance of the divine realm. I am being guided towards my highest good and towards fulfilling my soul's purpose. Thank you."

Archangel Uriel brings the message of enlightenment and understanding. He is known as the light of God and is associated with the sun. Uriel brings divine guidance and can help you see the truth in any situation. He can help you develop your intuition and connect with your inner wisdom. Uriel can also assist in releasing negative patterns and emotions, and help you find peace and forgiveness.

The message of Archangel Uriel is to trust in the divine plan and have faith that everything is happening for your highest good. He encourages you to let go of fear and doubt and to trust in the power of love.

Know that you are always supported and guided by the angels and the divine, even when you can't see it. Trust in the light within you and let it shine.

Archangel Uriel Mantra...

"Archangel Uriel, bring me clarity and wisdom. Help me to see the truth in all situations and guide me on my path towards spiritual enlightenment. I invite your divine presence to fill me with your loving energy and to protect me from any negative influences. Thank you for your loving support and guidance."

Archangel Azrael's divine message is one of comfort and transformation. Azrael reminds us that death is a natural part of life and encourages us to find peace and comfort in the face of loss and grief. The angel reminds us that those who have passed on are never truly gone and that they continue to watch over and guide us.

Azrael also reminds us of the transformative power of change and encourages us to embrace the process of transformation in our lives. The angel encourages us to let go of what no longer serves us and to trust in the wisdom of the universe as we navigate new beginnings and opportunities.

Overall, Archangel Azrael's message is one of comfort, transformation, and hope. The angel reminds us that even in the face of loss and change, we are never alone and that there is always hope for a brighter future.

Archangel Azrael Mantra...

"I find comfort in the face of loss and embrace the power of transformation."

By repeating this mantra, you can connect with Azrael's energy and find peace and comfort in the face of grief and loss. This mantra can also help you to embrace the process of transformation in your life and trust in the universe's plan for you.

Archangel Muriel is a gentle and compassionate angel who is known for her ability to bring peace and harmony into our lives. Her message for you today is to take time for self-care and to nurture your soul.

You may have been feeling stressed or overwhelmed lately, and it's important to prioritize your mental and emotional well-being. Take time to meditate, practice self-care, and surround yourself with positivity and love.

Call upon Archangel Muriel to help you release any negative energy or emotions that may be holding you back, and to bring peace and harmony into your life. Trust in her ability to guide you towards a state of inner peace and balance, and know that you are deserving of love and care.

Archangel Muriel Mantra...

"Archangel Muriel, thank you for your love and compassion. Please help me release any negative energy and emotions that are weighing me down. Surround me with your gentle energy and guide me towards a state of inner peace and harmony. I am open to receiving your healing light and love, and I trust in your ability to bring me comfort and joy. Thank you for your divine presence in my life."

Archangel Asariel's divine message is one of spiritual vision and clarity. Asariel reminds us of the importance of connecting with our inner wisdom and intuition to gain a deeper understanding of ourselves and the world around us. The angel encourages us to trust our instincts and to listen to the guidance of our higher selves.

Asariel also reminds us of the power of spiritual vision and the importance of setting intentions for our lives. The angel encourages us to focus our energy on our goals and dreams and to visualize ourselves achieving them.

Overall, Archangel Asariel's message is one of spiritual insight and vision. The angel reminds us to trust our inner wisdom, to set clear intentions for our lives, and to have faith that we are always guided towards our highest good.

Archangel Asariel Mantra...

"I trust my intuition and connect with my spiritual vision."

By repeating this mantra, you can connect with Asariel's energy and tap into your own intuition and inner wisdom. This mantra can help you to trust your instincts, gain clarity and insight, and set clear intentions for your life.

I am Archangel Raphael. I come to you today as a healer and a guide, ready to assist you in any way that I can. My love for you is infinite and unconditional, and I am always here for you whenever you need me.

Remember that healing is not just about physical wellness, but also about emotional, mental, and spiritual balance. Allow me to help you release any negative emotions or limiting beliefs that are holding you back from your full potential.

Know that you are a divine being, capable of achieving anything you set your mind to. Trust in the universe and have faith that everything is working out for your highest good.

Call upon me whenever you need assistance with healing, protection, or guidance. I am here to support you on your journey towards spiritual growth and enlightenment.

With love and light,

Archangel Raphael Mantra...

"I call upon Archangel Raphael to heal and guide me on my path. Thank you for your loving presence and divine protection."

By repeating this mantra, you can connect with Raphael's energy and cultivate a spirit of healing and guidance. This mantra can help you on your journey to spiritual awakedness with a loving heart.

Archangel Zaphkiel comes with a message of spiritual awakening, healing, and transformation. This powerful angel reminds you that you are not alone in your journey towards spiritual growth and that the divine realm is always here to support you.

Zaphkiel also reminds you to trust in the process of healing and transformation, even if it may be uncomfortable or difficult at times. The journey towards spiritual awakening is not always easy, but it is always worth it.

Finally, Zaphkiel encourages you to seek out opportunities for spiritual growth and to prioritize your spiritual practices. Whether it's through meditation, prayer, or other spiritual practices, make time for yourself to connect with the divine realm and to deepen your spiritual understanding.

Trust in the process of healing and transformation, seek out opportunities for spiritual growth, and prioritize your spiritual practices. Zaphkiel is here to guide and support you on your journey towards spiritual awakening and healing.

Archangel Zaphkiel Mantra...

"Archangel Zaphkiel, I trust in the process of healing and transformation. I invite your presence to fill me with the energy of spiritual awakening, healing, and transformation. I am deeply loved and supported by the divine realm. Thank you."

Archangel Michael is a powerful and protective angel who is known for his strength and courage. His message for you today is to trust in your own inner strength and to have faith in the universe's plan for you.

You may be facing challenges or obstacles on your path, but know that you have the power to overcome them. Call upon Archangel Michael for his protection and guidance, and trust in his ability to help you release any fears or doubts that may be holding you back.

Remember that you are a powerful and capable being, and that with the support of Archangel Michael and the universe, you can achieve anything you set your mind to. Stay true to yourself and your path, and trust that everything will work out for your highest good.

Archangel Michael Mantra...

"Archangel Michael, protect and guide me on my path. Fill me with your strength and courage, and help me release any fears or doubts. I trust in your power to keep me safe and to lead me towards my highest good. Thank you for your love and protection."

Archangel Ariel's divine message is one of nature, balance, and prosperity. Ariel reminds us of the importance of connecting with nature and finding balance in our lives. The angel encourages us to take time to appreciate the beauty of the natural world and to honour and protect the environment. Ariel also reminds us that abundance is our birthright and encourages us to open ourselves up to receive prosperity in all areas of our lives. The angel reminds us that by finding balance in our lives and connecting with the natural world, we can attract more abundance and prosperity into our lives.

Overall, Archangel Ariel's message is one of harmony and prosperity. The angel reminds us that by honouring the natural world and finding balance in our lives, we can create a more abundant and harmonious world for ourselves and others.

Archangel Ariel Mantra...

"I am connected to nature, in harmony with the universe, and open to receiving abundance."

By repeating this mantra, you can connect with Ariel's energy and feel a sense of balance, harmony, and abundance in your life. This mantra can help you to ground yourself in nature, honour the environment, and attract prosperity in all areas of your life.

Archangel Daniel's divine message is one of strength and courage. Daniel reminds us that we are capable of overcoming any obstacle or challenge that comes our way, and encourages us to tap into our inner strength and resilience.

The angel also reminds us of the importance of staying true to ourselves and our values, even in the face of adversity. Daniel encourages us to stand up for what we believe in and to have the courage to speak our truth, even if it may be difficult.

Overall, Archangel Daniel's message is one of strength, courage, and faith. The angel reminds us that we have the inner strength and resilience to overcome any challenge, and encourages us to stay true to ourselves and trust in the universe's plan. So, we should have faith in ourselves and in the divine plan.

Archangel Daniel Mantra...
"I am strong, courageous, and supported by the angels and the universe."

By repeating this mantra, you can connect with Daniel's energy and tap into a sense of inner strength and resilience. This mantra can also help you to stay true to your values and beliefs, and to have the courage to speak your truth.

Archangel Israfil's divine message is one of harmony, music, and divine order. The angel reminds us that every living being has a unique role to play in the grand scheme of the universe and that all of creation is interconnected.

Israfil also encourages us to embrace the power of music and sound as a way to connect with the divine. By listening to and creating music, we can tap into the universal language of the cosmos and feel a sense of oneness with all of creation.

Israfil encourages us to trust in the unfolding of our lives, even when things don't make sense at the moment.

Overall, Archangel Israfil's message is one of harmony, music, and divine order. The angel reminds us to embrace our unique role in the universe, connect with the power of music and sound, and trust in the divine order of the universe.

Archangel Israphil Mantra...

"I embrace the power of music and divine order, and trust in my unique role in the universe."

By repeating this mantra, you can connect with Israfil's energy and tap into the power of music and divine order in your life. This mantra can also help you to trust in your unique role in the universe and embrace the interconnectedness of all of creation.

Archangel Ramiel brings a message of hope and renewal. He reminds us that even in the darkest moments, there is always a light shining within us. He encourages us to trust in ourselves and our abilities, to believe in our dreams, and to take action towards manifesting them.

Ramiel also reminds us of the importance of forgiveness, both towards others and ourselves. Holding onto grudges and past hurts only weighs us down and prevent us from moving forward. By releasing these negative emotions and embracing forgiveness, we can open ourselves up to new opportunities and experiences.

Through Ramiel's message, we are reminded that we are powerful beings capable of creating the life we desire. By tapping into our inner strength, letting go of the past, and forgiving ourselves and others, we can manifest our deepest desires and live a fulfilling life.

Archangel Ramiel Mantra...

"I trust in my inner light and forgive with an open heart. I am capable of creating the life I desire."

By repeating this mantra, you can connect with Ramiel's energy and cultivate a spirit of hope, and renewal. This mantra can help you to remain open to new opportunities and possibilities.

Archangel Barachiel's divine message is one of joy and blessings. Barachiel reminds us that we are loved and supported by the universe, and encourages us to embrace the blessings that surround us every day. The angel reminds us to find joy in the present moment and to express gratitude for all that we have.

Barachiel also reminds us of the importance of helping others and encourages us to spread love and kindness wherever we go. The angel reminds us that by lifting others up, we also lift ourselves up, and that our kindness can have a ripple effect that extends far beyond ourselves.

Overall, Archangel Barachiel's message is one of joy, gratitude, and service. The angel reminds us to embrace the blessings in our lives, find joy in the present moment, and spread love and kindness wherever we go.

Archangel Barachiel Mantra...
"I am surrounded by blessings and joy, and I spread love and kindness wherever I go."

By repeating this mantra, you can connect with Barachiel's energy and invite blessings and joy into your life. This mantra can also help you to cultivate a spirit of gratitude and service, as you focus on spreading love and kindness to others.

Archangel Jerahmeel's divine message is one of hope and encouragement. The angel reminds us that even in our darkest moments, there is always a glimmer of light and a path forward.

Jerahmeel also encourages us to be open to new opportunities and possibilities and to have faith in ourselves and our abilities. By stepping outside of our comfort zones and taking risks, we can discover new talents and abilities, and experience growth and transformation.

Finally, Jerahmeel reminds us of the importance of compassion and kindness towards ourselves and others. When we extend love and understanding to ourselves and those around us, we create a more peaceful and harmonious world.

Overall, Archangel Jerahmeel's message is one of hope, faith, and compassion. The angel encourages us to be open to new possibilities, have faith in ourselves, and extend love and kindness to ourselves and others.

Archangel Jerahmeel Mantra...
"I am open to new possibilities. I have faith in myself, and I extend love and kindness to myself and others."

By repeating this mantra, you can connect with Jerahmeel's energy and cultivate a spirit of hope, faith, and compassion. This mantra can help you to remain open to new opportunities and possibilities.

Archangel Metatron is a powerful and wise angel who oversees the flow of divine energy and spiritual knowledge. His message for you today is to remember that you are a divine being with infinite potential and the power to co-create your reality.

Take a moment to connect with your inner wisdom and tune into the guidance of the universe. Trust that you are exactly where you are meant to be, and that everything is unfolding in divine timing.

Remember that you are never alone and that Archangel Metatron and your other spirit guides are always with you, ready to offer guidance and support. Trust in the universe, believe in yourself, and know that you are capable of achieving all of your dreams and aspirations.

Archangel Metatron Mantra...

"Divine Metatron, please guide me to align with my highest path and purpose. Help me to connect with my inner wisdom and intuition, and to trust in the universe's plan for me. Please infuse me with the wisdom and knowledge I need to navigate this journey with grace and ease."

Archangel Zuriel comes with a message of strength, courage, and perseverance. This powerful angel reminds you that you have the strength and inner power to overcome any obstacles that may come your way. You are capable of achieving your goals and fulfilling your dreams, even if the path may be challenging.

Zuriel also reminds you to have courage and to take bold steps towards your dreams. You may feel fear or doubt at times, but remember that the divine realm is here to support you and to guide you towards your highest good.

Finally, Zuriel encourages you to persevere in the face of adversity. Keep moving forward towards your goals, and trust that the universe is conspiring in your favor.

You have the strength, courage, and perseverance to achieve your goals and fulfill your dreams. Zuriel is here to guide and support you on your journey towards success and fulfillment.

Archangel Zuriel Mantra...

"Archangel Zuriel, I embrace my inner strength and power. I have the courage to take bold steps towards my dreams, even if the path may be challenging. I invite your presence to fill me with the energy of strength, courage, and perseverance. I am deeply loved and supported by the divine realm. Thank you."

Archangel Haniel's divine message is one of intuition, balance, and grace. The angel reminds us to trust our intuition and to listen to our inner wisdom, even when it goes against the opinions of others or societal norms.

Haniel also encourages us to seek balance in all areas of our lives, whether it be in our relationships, work, or personal growth. The angel reminds us that by finding balance, we can experience greater peace and harmony in our lives.

Haniel reminds us of the importance of grace and forgiveness, both towards ourselves and others. The angel encourages us to let go of any resentment or bitterness we may be holding onto and to embrace a mindset of love and compassion.

Overall, Archangel Haniel's message is one of intuition, balance, and grace. The angel reminds us to trust ourselves, seek balance, and let go of negativity in order to live a more fulfilling and peaceful life.

Archangel Haniel Mantra...

"I trust my intuition and find balance and grace in all areas of my life."

By repeating this mantra, you can connect with Haniel's energy and tap into your own intuition and inner wisdom. This mantra can also help you to seek balance and find grace in all areas of your life, bringing greater peace and harmony.

Archangel Chazagiel's divine message is one of creativity and inspiration. Chazagiel reminds us that we all have unique talents and gifts, and encourages us to tap into our creativity and express ourselves in new and innovative ways. The angel also reminds us that inspiration can come from unexpected places, and encourages us to remain open and receptive to new ideas and experiences.

Chazagiel also reminds us of the importance of self-care and taking time to nourish our creative spirit. The angel encourages us to prioritize the things that bring us joy and inspiration, and to make time for creative pursuits in our daily lives.

Overall, Archangel Chazagiel's message is one of creativity, inspiration, and self-care. The angel reminds us to tap into our unique gifts and talents, stay open to new ideas and experiences, and prioritize self-care in order to nourish our creative spirit.

Archangel Chazagiel Mantra...
"I am open to receiving inspiration and expressing my unique creative gifts."

By repeating this mantra, you can connect with Chazagiel's energy and tap into a sense of openness and creativity. This mantra can also help you to remain receptive to new ideas and experiences, and to prioritize self-care and creative pursuits in your daily life.

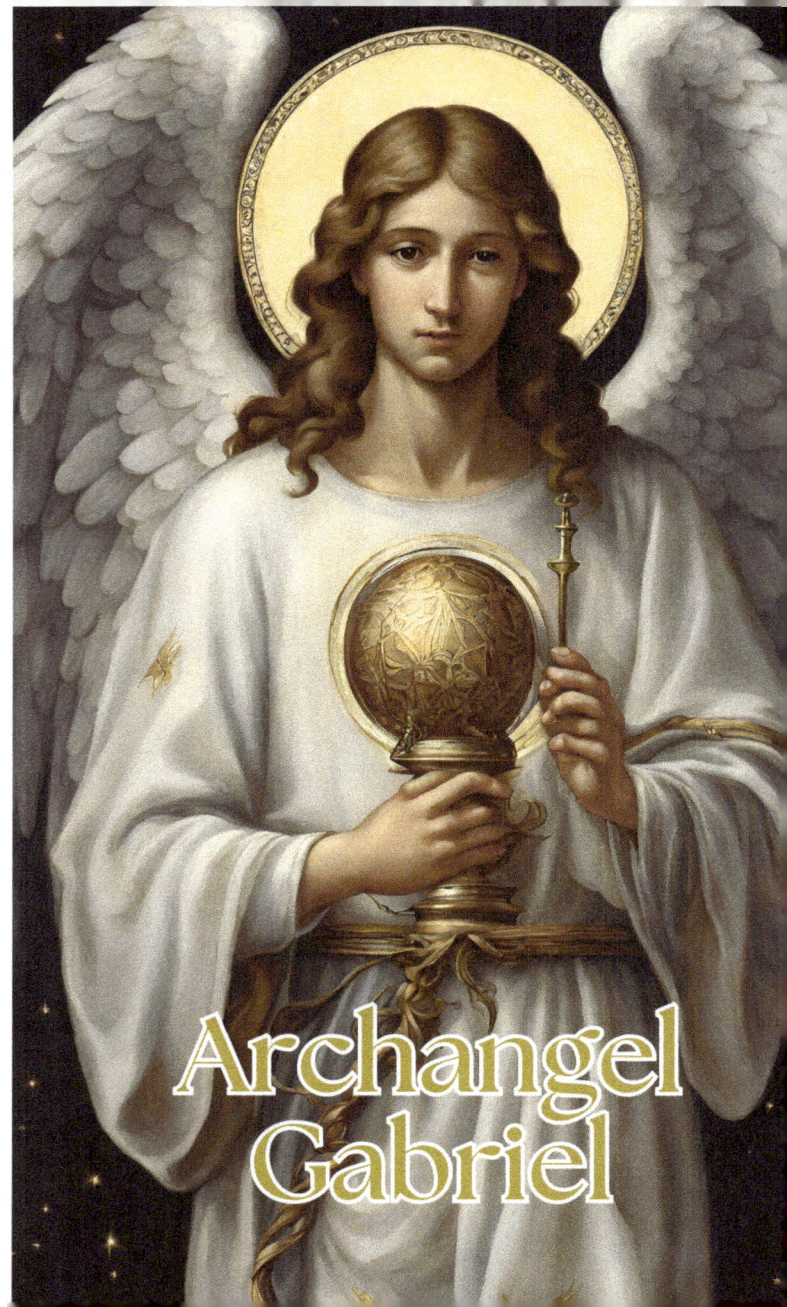

Archangel Gabriel's divine message is one of communication and creativity. Gabriel reminds us that we all have a unique voice and creative gifts, and encourages us to use them to inspire and uplift others.

The angel also reminds us of the importance of clear communication in all areas of our lives, whether it be in our personal relationships or in our work. Gabriel encourages us to speak our truth with love and compassion and to listen to others with an open mind and heart.

Overall, Archangel Gabriel's message is one of creativity, communication, and connection. The angel reminds us of the power of our words and actions, and encourages us to use them to inspire and uplift others. So, we should use our creativity and communication skills to make a positive impact on the world around us.

Archangel Gabriel Mantra...
"I am open to receiving divine inspiration and guidance, and I trust in my creative abilities."

By repeating this mantra, you can connect with Gabriel's energy and tap into your own creativity and intuition. This mantra can also help you to communicate more clearly and effectively with others.

Archangel Jophiel's divine message is one of beauty, creativity, and inspiration. The angel reminds us to seek and appreciate the beauty in our surroundings, both in nature and in the people around us. By doing so, we can cultivate a sense of gratitude and joy in our lives.

Jophiel also encourages us to tap into our own creative energy, whether through art, music, writing, or any other form of self-expression. When we allow ourselves to express our creativity, we tap into our inner wisdom and connect with our highest selves.

Finally, Jophiel reminds us to seek inspiration from the divine, whether through prayer, meditation, or simply taking time to connect with our spiritual selves.

Overall, Archangel Jophiel's message is one of beauty, creativity, and spiritual connection. The angel encourages us to seek and appreciate the beauty in our surroundings, tap into our own creative energy, and connect with the divine.

Archangel Jophiel Mantra...

" I am open to receiving divine inspiration. I trust in the guidance and support of Archangel Jophiel to help me see the beauty in all things."

Repeat this mantra whenever you need a reminder to connect with the energy of Archangel Jophiel. Allow the angel's energy to uplift and inspire you.

Archangel Phanuel, brings you a message of hope and renewal.

The divine light of the universe is shining upon you, guiding you towards your highest potential. Know that you are loved and supported and that your angels are always by your side. Trust in the path that is unfolding before you, and have faith that everything is happening for your highest good.

Allow yourself to let go of any fears or doubts, and embrace the infinite possibilities that are available to you.

Remember that you are a powerful co-creator of your reality, and that your thoughts and actions have the power to shape your future. Trust in your own inner wisdom, and know that you are capable of creating a life filled with joy, love, and abundance.

Archangel Phanuel Mantra...
"Phanuel, I call upon your divine presence to guide me towards my purpose and destiny. Help me let go of any doubts and fears that may be holding me back and grant me the courage and strength to face any challenges that come my way. So be it, and so it is."

Archangel Verchial comes with a message of abundance, prosperity, and manifestation. This powerful angel reminds you that you are a co-creator of your reality and that you have the power to manifest your dreams into existence. Trust in the Universe and know that you are fully supported in your endeavors.

Verchial also reminds you to stay focused and committed to your goals. Don't let doubts or fears hold you back, for they are only illusions.

Finally, Verchial encourages you to be of service to others, to share your abundance and blessings with those in need. By doing so, you not only uplift others, but you also raise your own vibration and attract even more blessings into your life. Trust in the abundance of the Universe and know that you are deeply loved and supported by Verchial and the divine realm.

Archangel Verchial Mantra...

"Archangel Verchial, I trust in the abundance of the Universe. I am a co-creator of my reality and I manifest my dreams into existence. I stay focused and committed to my goals, knowing that I am fully supported by the divine realm. I express gratitude for all the blessings in my life and share my abundance with those in need. Thank you for your loving guidance and support."

Archangel Cornucopia's divine message is one of abundance and prosperity. Cornucopia reminds us that we are worthy of abundance and that it is our birthright. The angel encourages us to focus on what we have, rather than what we lack, and to cultivate an attitude of gratitude for all that we have been given.

Cornucopia also reminds us that abundance comes in many forms, not just material wealth. It can come in the form of love, joy, and meaningful relationships. The angel encourages us to open our hearts to receive all the abundance that the universe has to offer.

Overall, Archangel Cornucopia's message is one of hope and encouragement. The angel reminds us that abundance is available to us all, and that we simply need to open ourselves up to receive it.

Archangel Cornucopia Mantra...
"I am worthy of abundance in all areas of my life."

By repeating this mantra, you can connect with Cornucopia's energy and open yourself up to receive all the abundance that the universe has to offer. It can help you shift your focus away from lack and towards gratitude, allowing you to attract more abundance into your life.

Archangel Zephaniel comes with a message of creativity, inspiration, and self-expression. This powerful angel reminds you that you are a unique and creative being, with a special gift to offer the world. It's time to let go of any fears or doubts and to embrace your creativity and self-expression.

Zephaniel also reminds you to take time for yourself, to nurture your creativity and to connect with your inner self. By doing so, you can access your deepest inspirations and bring forth your most authentic self.

Finally, Zephaniel encourages you to share your creativity and self-expression with others. You have the power to inspire and uplift those around you, and to make a positive impact on the world.

Embrace your creativity and self-expression, take time for yourself to nurture your gifts, and share your unique talents with the world. Zephaniel is here to guide and support you on your journey towards creative fulfillment and self-expression.

Archangel Zephaniel Mantra...

"Archangel Zephaniel, I embrace my creativity and self-expression. I let go of any fears or doubts and trust in my unique gifts and talents. I invite your presence to fill me with the energy of creativity, inspiration, and self-expression. I am deeply loved and supported by the divine realm. Thank you."

Archangel Raziel is known as the angel of divine secrets and knowledge. His message for you today is that you are ready to receive the knowledge and wisdom that the universe has to offer. Be open to the signs and messages that are being sent your way, as they are guiding you towards your true purpose.

You have been called to walk the path of spiritual awakening and it is important that you stay true to your inner self. You may feel overwhelmed at times, but trust that everything is happening for your highest good.

Raziel reminds you that you are a powerful co-creator of your reality and that your thoughts and intentions have the power to manifest into reality. Stay focused on what you truly desire and watch as the universe conspires to bring it into fruition.

Archangel Raziel Mantra...

"Archangel Raziel, I call upon your divine wisdom and guidance. Help me connect with the knowledge and insights of the universe"

Repeat this mantra as often as you like to connect with Archangel Raziel and invite his wisdom and guidance into your life. Remember to also listen to your intuition and remain open to receiving insights and messages from the universe.

Archangel Sachiel, brings you a message of hope and abundance. The universe is abundant, and you are a divine being with the power to manifest your desires. Trust in yourself and in the power of the universe to provide for you. Remember to express gratitude for all that you already have and trust that more is on the way.

As you navigate through life's challenges, call upon me for guidance and support. I am here to assist you in finding the courage and strength to overcome any obstacles in your path. Trust that you are never alone, and we angels are always here to guide and support you.

Believe in yourself, and trust in the universe. Abundance and blessings are on their way to you.

Archangel Sachiel Mantra...

"Divine Archangel Sachiel, I call upon you now, Please bring to me abundance, prosperity and flow, Clear any blocks or obstacles that I may face, And guide me towards opportunities that lead to grace. Thank you for your loving presence and support, I am open to receive all that you may report. With gratitude and trust, I release this prayer, Knowing that all my needs are met with ease and care."

Archangel Adabiel's divine message is one of hope and inspiration. Adabiel reminds us that we are capable of achieving our dreams and that we have the power within us to make them a reality. The angel encourages us to believe in ourselves and to trust that the universe will support us on our journey.

Adabiel also reminds us that every challenge we face is an opportunity for growth and learning. The angel encourages us to embrace these challenges and to use them as stepping stones towards our goals.

Overall, Archangel Adabiel's message is one of empowerment and encouragement. The angel reminds us that we are not alone on our journey and that we have the support of the universe behind us. By believing in ourselves and staying focused on our goals, we can achieve anything we set our minds to.

Archangel Adabiel Mantra...
"I am capable and supported in achieving my dreams."

By repeating this mantra, you can connect with Adabiel's energy and draw upon the angel's strength and inspiration. This mantra can help you stay focused on your goals and remind you that you have the power within you to make them a reality.

Archangel Camael's divine message is one of strength and courage. Camael reminds us that we are capable of overcoming any challenge or obstacle in our path and encourages us to have faith in our strengths and abilities. The angel reminds us that we are never alone in our struggles and that we can always call upon the angels for guidance and support.

Camael also reminds us of the importance of standing up for what we believe in and speaking our truth with confidence and courage. The angel encourages us to trust in our intuition and follow our heart, even in the face of opposition or doubt.

Overall, Archangel Camael's message is one of strength, courage, and conviction. The angel reminds us to have faith in our power, call upon the angels for support, and stand up for what we believe in.

Archangel Camael Mantra…

"I am strong, courageous, and capable of overcoming any obstacle."

By repeating this mantra, you can connect with Camael's energy and tap into your own inner strength and courage. This mantra can also help you to trust in your own abilities and have faith in your path, even in the face of challenges or obstacles.

Archangel Uziel comes with a message of strength, courage, and perseverance. This powerful angel reminds you that you have the inner strength and wisdom to overcome any challenges or obstacles that come your way.

Uziel also reminds you to stay focused on your path and to remain true to yourself. Don't let outside influences or the opinions of others sway you from your true purpose. Trust in your intuition and inner guidance, and have the courage to follow your heart.

Finally, Uziel encourages you to take action and make positive changes in your life. Don't be afraid to step outside of your comfort zone and try new things. You have the support and guidance of the divine realm, and you are never alone.

Trust in yourself, stay focused on your goals, and have the courage to take action. Uziel is here to guide and support you on your journey.

Archangel Uziel Mantra...

"Archangel Uziel, I trust in my own inner strength and wisdom. I have the courage and perseverance to overcome any challenges that come my way. I stay true to myself and trust in my intuition and inner guidance. I take action and make positive changes in my life, knowing that I am supported and guided by the divine realm."

Archangel Zacharial comes with a message of healing, forgiveness, and compassion. This powerful angel reminds you that true healing can only come from a place of love and forgiveness. It's time to let go of any grudges or resentments you may be holding onto and to open your heart to forgiveness and compassion.

Zacharial also reminds you to take care of yourself, both physically and emotionally. It's important to nurture yourself and to practice self-care in order to maintain your overall well-being. This includes setting healthy boundaries and taking time for yourself to recharge and rejuvenate.

Finally, Zacharial encourages you to be of service to others, to offer a helping hand to those in need and to spread love and kindness wherever you go. By doing so, you not only uplift others, but you also raise your own vibration and attract even more blessings into your life.

Trust in the power of healing, forgiveness, and compassion. Zacharial is here to guide and support you on your journey towards inner peace and well-being.

Archangel Zacherial Mantra...

"Archangel Zacherial, I invite your presence to fill me with the energy of healing, forgiveness, and compassion. I trust in the power of love and know that I am deeply loved and supported by the divine realm. Thank you"

Archangel Ananiel's divine message is one of spiritual growth and self-discovery. Ananiel reminds us of the importance of connecting with our higher selves and deepening our spiritual practices. The angel encourages us to take time for self-reflection, meditate, and explore our spiritual beliefs and practices.

Ananiel also reminds us that we are never alone on our spiritual journey and that the angels and the universe are always with us, guiding us towards our highest good. The angel encourages us to trust in the process of our spiritual growth and to have faith that everything is unfolding exactly as it should.

Overall, Archangel Ananiel's message is one of trust and guidance. The angel reminds us to connect with our spiritual selves and to trust in the wisdom of the universe as we navigate our spiritual journeys.

Archangel Ananiel Mantra...
"I trust in my spiritual journey and have faith in the universe."

By repeating this mantra, you can connect with Ananiel's energy and feel supported on your spiritual journey. This mantra can help you release any fears or doubts you may have and remind you to trust in the process of your spiritual growth.

Archangel Raguel brings a message of harmony and balance. He reminds us that every relationship, whether it be with others or with ourselves, is a sacred and precious bond that should be nurtured with care and respect.

He encourages us to seek out peaceful resolutions to conflicts, to forgive ourselves and others, and to strive for fairness and justice in all our interactions. Through his loving guidance, we can learn to let go of anger, bitterness, and resentment, and instead, cultivate compassion, empathy, and understanding.

Trust in his presence to help bring order and balance to any situation, and to heal any wounds that may have caused discord or disharmony in our lives.

Archangel Raguel Mantra...

"Archangel Raguel, I invite your presence to bring peace and harmony to my relationships and within myself. Help me to let go of any anger or resentment, and to forgive myself and others. I ask for your guidance in finding a peaceful resolution to any conflicts and bringing fairness and justice to all my interactions. Thank you for your loving guidance and healing, and for bringing balance and harmony to my life. So be it, and so it is."

Archangel Cassiel's divine message is one of patience and perseverance. Cassiel reminds us that everything happens in divine timing and that our current circumstances are part of a larger plan. The angel encourages us to trust in the universe and have faith that everything will work out for our highest good.

Cassiel also reminds us of the importance of taking responsibility for our actions and learning from our mistakes. The angel encourages us to have patience with ourselves and to keep moving forward, even when the path is difficult.

Overall, Archangel Cassiel's message is one of patience, perseverance, and trust. The angel reminds us to have faith in the universe and trust in our path, even when it may be challenging. The angel also encourages us to take responsibility for our actions and keep moving forward, one step at a time.

Archangel Cassiel Mantra...
"I trust in the universe's divine timing, and I have patience and perseverance on my path."

By repeating this mantra, you can connect with Cassiel's energy and tap into a sense of trust and patience. This mantra can also help you to stay focused on your goals and keep moving forward, even when the path is challenging.

The Answers You Seek

Are Within

My daily thoughts....

My daily thoughts....

My daily thoughts....

My daily thoughts....

My daily thoughts....

My daily thoughts....

My daily thoughts....

My daily thoughts....

My daily thoughts....

My daily thoughts....

My daily thoughts....

My daily thoughts....

My daily thoughts....

My daily thoughts....

My daily thoughts....

My daily thoughts....

My daily thoughts....

My daily thoughts....

Amanda Clarke, the acclaimed author of "Divine Guidance: Answers from the Oracles," returns with "Messages from the Angels: Guidance and Inspiration from Divine Messengers." This book is a vibrant testament to Amanda's profound connection with the universe and her commitment to providing a simple yet powerful means of accessing divine guidance.

Drawing from her rich background in spirituality, mysticism, and personal growth, Amanda deepens her exploration into the spiritual realm, guiding readers to communicate directly with the celestial. "Messages from the Angels" extends beyond a typical collection of wisdom; it serves as a sacred link, connecting readers with the divine through the voices of 34 archangels.

Amanda highlights the importance of the relationship readers can develop with the book. It is envisioned not just as a guide, but as a spiritual companion, responsive to the unique vibrations of each individual. She promotes a process of simplicity—hold the book, meditate upon its contents, and channel personal energy into its pages, transforming the reading into a deeply personal and intimate experience.

As readers delve into "Messages from the Angels," Amanda's aspiration is that each person will discover solace, clarity, and profound inspiration. The book is crafted not merely as a guide but as an open invitation to forge a deep connection with the divine, navigate the complexities of life's queries, and embark on a transformative path of self-discovery.

Namaste—The divine in me honors the divine in you, inviting you to join in this celestial journey.

More on the Bookshelves at www.korupublishing.com

www.ingramcontent.com/pod-product-compliance
Lightning Source LLC
Chambersburg PA
CBHW062040290426
44109CB00026B/2689